Encouragement

THE ABC's

APPRECIATION · TOUCH · TRUST · IMAGINATION

TIME · UNDERSTANDING · DIRECTION

ENTHUSIASM

A

IS FOR ATTITUDE

Copyright Information

Visit Curt Goad's website at www.curtgoad.com

Mr. Encouragement is a registered trademark of Curt Goad Ministries, Inc.

Encouragement, the ABC's, A is for Attitude

Book design and production by Kim Parrish Creative Services, Inc.
www.kimparrishcreative.com

To

_____

From

_____

Date

_____

FORWARD

Welcome! This book is the first of 26 books of *ENCOURAGEMENT, THE ABC's*. I have found that life can be better with encouragement. Giving encouragement is a gift that has been given to me and I love passing it on to others. That is why they call me "Mr. Encouragement".

My goal is for the reader to laugh, refresh their outlook on life and know that there is hope as they read this easy book of quotes, stories and humor. The book is short, as one of the things I tell my audiences when I speak … my grandfather used to tell me you need to give a speech like a woman's skirt … short enough to keep their attention, but long enough to cover the subject matter. Enjoy! Be Encouraged and look forward to *B is for BLESSED!*

Have a great day, it's yours to enjoy!
Curt Goad

The largest room in the house is the room for self improvement.

Contents

INTRODUCTION............................. 1

APPRECIATION........................... 9

TOUCH................................... 19

TRUST................................... 25

IMAGINATION.......................... 35

TIME.................................... 41

UNDERSTANDING.................... 57

DIRECTION............................. 67

ENTHUSIASM.......................... 75

Attitude

An Introduction

You may have heard that your attitude is everything. I agree. It always helps me to have a booster shot when it comes to my attitude and these nuggets remind me to have a great attitude!

- Your attitude is contagious. Is yours worth catching?

- Most peoples attitude is like concrete, all mixed up and permanently set. *–Zig Zigler*

- If you don't like something change it; if you can't change something, change your attitude about it. *–Maya Angelou*

- Life is full of changes and you have to deal with it. Change before you have to.

- Fear is just excitement that needs an attitude adjustment. *–Russ Quaglia*

- Which is worse crying over spilled milk or keeping everything bottled up?

Remember, you're valuable not because of what you do, but because of who you are.

As a man thinketh in his heart so is he.
Proverbs 23:7
KJV

- If you settle for what's good, you'll never have what's best, because the biggest enemy of best is good.

- Nurture your mind with great thoughts because you will never go higher than you think. *—Benjamin Disraeli*

- Your thoughts have a voice too.

- Remember, your head is not just there to keep your ears apart and hold your hair up. It's the only part of your body that God gave you total control over.

- Always have the attitude, "Hang in there, don't give up. Your best days are ahead of you."

- Your attitude is not simply a state of mind. It is what you value.

Happiness is not having the best of everything, it is making the best of everything.

- It's never the right time to do the wrong thing.

- You live only once, but once is enough if you live it right.

- Doing the job is an accomplishment. Doing the job right is an achievement.

- You don't need to be great to start, but you have to start to be great.

- Turn your "should do" list into your "must do" list.

- If you don't have anything good to say about somebody, don't say it. Make sure your words are sweet, because someday you may need to eat them.

The tongue weighs very little, but most people aren't strong enough to hold it.

I believe there are basically three types of attitudes that people have in life:

1. Painful hostility: they start on the bottom and that's where they think they will stay forever. They have the most expensive party in the world, a pity party. Erma Bombeck said, "If life is such a bowl of cherries, why am I always in the pits." That is where the word pitiful comes from.

2. Peaceful coexistence: they could do better, but they settle for where they are in life.

3. Passionate interest: this is what we all strive for. Don't give up, do whatever it takes. Why settle for the ordinary when God has designed something extraordinary for you. If you hang in there and don't give up, your best days are ahead of you.

Your attitude is a daily decision. Governors on cars are a mechanical devise that keep the car from reaching its full potential. Take the governors off of your life. Make it a great day!

H ere is a story that sums up attitude and gives a great example of what to strive for:

The 92-year-old petite, well-poised and proud lady, who is fully dressed each morning by eight o'clock, with her hair fashionably coifed and makeup perfectly applied, even though she is legally blind, moved to a nursing home today. Her husband of 70 years recently passed away, making the move necessary.

After many hours of waiting patiently in the lobby of the nursing home, she smiled sweetly when told her room was ready. As she maneuvered her walker to the elevator, I provided a visual description of her tiny room, including the eyelet sheets that had been hung on her window.

"I love it," she stated with the enthusiasm of an eight-year old having just been presented with a new puppy.

I said "Mrs. Jones, you haven't seen the room, just wait."

"That doesn't have anything to do with it," she replied.

"Happiness is something you decide on ahead of time. Whether I like my room or not doesn't depend on how the furniture is arranged … it's how I arrange my mind. I already decided to love it. It's a decision I make every morning when I wake up. I have a choice: I can spend the day in bed recounting the difficulty I have with the parts of my body that no longer work, or get out of bed and be thankful for the ones that do. Each day is a gift, and as long as my eyes open, I'll focus on the new day and all the happy memories I've stored away … just for this time in my life."

When you are down and out and know your attitude needs a lift … remember Mrs. Jones and focus on the good things.

Appreciation

Touch

Trust

Imagination

Time

Understanding

Direction

Enthusiasm

Appreciation

I ask people all the time, "2-4-6-8 what do you appreciate about me?" They laugh, and I know they do appreciate me. Try it. Appreciation is like fertilizer, it helps you grow.

The first step to appreciation is gratitude. If you develop and heighten your powers of appreciation by focusing on the beauty in your life, instead of the imperfections, you will be halfway there. I guarantee that you will see an abundance of beauty in your life, regardless of your surroundings or circumstances, if you will only look for it.

People need the three A's; attention, appreciation and affection. Give appreciation, watch others beam and find out that you yourself have grown.

The way to develop the best that is in a man is by appreciation and encouragement.

—*Charles Schwab*

Chapter 1

For beautiful eyes, look for the good in others; for beautiful lips, speak only words of kindness; and for poise, walk with the knowledge that you are never alone. *–Audrey Hepburn*

Write a letter of appreciation to the people who have changed your life: a teacher, a preacher, a special friend, family members … the list is endless.

You have it easily in your power to increase the sum total of this world's happiness now. How? By giving a few words of sincere appreciation to someone who is lonely or discouraged. Perhaps you will forget tomorrow the kind words you say today, but the recipient may cherish them over a lifetime. *–Dale Carnegie*

Once we discover how to appreciate the timeless values in our daily experiences, we can enjoy the best things in life. *–Harry Hepner*

There are highlights in all of our lives and most of them have come about through encouragement from someone else. I don't care how great, how famous, or how successful a man or woman may be ... each hungers for applause.

We all need a little RAP – Recognition ... Appreciation ... Praise.

Encouragement is oxygen to the soul. Work can never be expected from a worker without encouragement ... no one has ever lived without it.
–*George Matthew Adams*

Appreciation is like salt – a little goes a long way bringing out the best in us.

The way to develop the best that is in a man is by appreciation and encouragement.
–*Charles Schwab*

12

Chapter 1

How I Describe My Friends

1. In **first grade** your idea of a good friend was the person who went to the bathroom with you and held your hand as you walked through the scary halls.

2. In **second grade** your idea of a good friend was the person who helped you stand up to the class bully.

3. In **third grade** your idea of a good friend was the person who shared their lunch with you when you left yours on the bus.

4. In **fourth grade** your idea of a good friend was the person who was willing to switch square dancing partners in gym so you wouldn't have to be stuck do-si-do-ing with Nasty Nicky or Smelly Susan.

5. In **fifth grade** your idea of a friend was the person who saved a seat in the back of the bus for you.

13

6. In **sixth grade** your idea of a friend was the person who went up to Nick or Susan, your new crush, and asked them to dance with you. (So that if they said no you wouldn't have to be embarrassed.)

7. In **seventh grade** your idea of a friend was the person who let you copy the social studies homework from the night before that you had forgotten to do.

8. In **eighth grade** your idea of a good friend was the person who helped you pack up your stuffed animals and old baseball cards so that your room would be a "high schooler's" room, but didn't laugh at you when you finished and broke out into tears.

9. In **ninth grade** your idea of a good friend was the person who went to that "cool" party thrown by a senior so you wouldn't wind up being the only freshman there.

10. In **tenth grade** your idea of a good friend was the person who changed his or her schedule so you would have someone to sit with at lunch.

11. In **eleventh grade** your idea of a good friend was the person who gave you rides in their new car, convinced your parents that you shouldn't be grounded, consoled you when you broke up with Nick or Susan, and found you a date to the prom.

12. In **twelfth grade** your idea of a good friend was the person who helped you pick out a college or what you would do next, assured you that you would get into that college, or move onto your next job, and helped you deal with your parents who were having a hard time adjusting to the idea of letting you go.

13. At **graduation** your idea of a good friend was the person who was crying on the inside but managed the biggest smile one could give as they congratulated you.

Give appreciation,
watch others
beam and find out
that you yourself
have grown.

Chapter 1

Now your idea of a good friend is still the person who gives you the better of the two choices, holds your hand when you're scared, helps you fight off those who try to take advantage of you, thinks of you at times when you are not there, reminds you of what you have forgotten, helps you put the past behind you, but understands when you need to hold on to it a little longer, stays with you so that you have confidence, goes out of their way to make time for you, helps you clear up your mistakes, helps you deal with pressure from others, smiles for you when they are sad, and helps you become a better person. I hope this helps you think of who are great friends and secondly, appreciate them! *–Author Unknown*

Appreciation

Touch

Trust

Imagination

Time

Understanding

Direction

Enthusiasm

CHAPTER 2
Touch

Have you ever considered the power of a handshake? It is said when two hands meet we pass on something of ourselves. After being introduced to Mark Twain, Helen Keller commented, "I can feel the twinkle of his eye in his handshake." Transfer part of yourself to others and allow them to transfer part of themselves to you. Both of you will be better for it!

Reach out and touch someone … you may remember that from a commercial for AT&T years ago. But there is so much truth to that … you should try it!

When you look at your hand, it can help you remember who you should reach out and touch.

- Your thumb is nearest to you. Touch those that are closest to you.

- The next finger is the pointing finger. Touch those that teach, instruct and heal.
- The next finger is the tallest finger. Touch the leaders in your life.
- The fourth finger is our ring finger, which surprisingly, is the weakest, to remind us of those in our lives that are weak, in trouble or pain.
- Lastly, the smallest finger and that's where you should place yourself in relation to God and others. *–Author Unknown*

One touch from you can change anything. One touch of God's hand can change everything.

Don't be discouraged at His pruning touch. God is constantly at work in the lives of those He plans to use greatly.

Encouragement is like a pebble thrown into water. While there is always an immediate impact, the ripples continue indefinitely. You will never know what will happen with that kind word, that written note, that warm touch you give to a grieving, hurting person. Your ripples could start something that will never end.

One touch of God's hand can change everything.

If you can hold someone's hand, hug them or even touch them on the shoulder … you are blessed because you can offer healing touch.

Stay in touch, stay informed, stay involved.

If we are to really live, there must be an unhindered out-flow of our time, energy, and money – our very lives in touching and blessing the lives of others.

Heartprints

Whatever our hands touch---
We leave fingerprints!

On walls, on furniture,
On doorknobs, dishes, books,
As we touch we leave our identity.

Oh, please, wherever I go today,
Help me leave heartprints!
Heartprints of compassion
Of understanding and love.
Heartprints of kindness
And genuine concern.

May my heart touch a lonely neighbor,
Or a runaway daughter,
Or an anxious mother,
Or, perhaps, a dear friend!

I shall go out today
To leave heartprints,
And if someone should say
"I felt your touch,"
May that one sense be … YOUR LOVE
Touching through ME …

—Author unknown

*"May the love of the Lord
touch everything you do and remind you
you're forever blessed."*

A ppreciation

T ouch

T rust

I magination

T ime

U nderstanding

D irection

E nthusiasm

Trust

Trust is the emotional glue that bonds leaders and followers together.
—*Warren Bennis and Burt Nanus*

Fire, water and trust were walking in the woods, they were talking about what should happen if they got separated from each other. Fire said, "You'll know where I am because you will see the smoke." Water said, "You'll know where I am because the grass will be green and the flowers will be blooming." Trust said, "You better never lose me, because if you lose me you might never find me again."

Trust is something that takes a lifetime to build and maintain, but it only takes a second to destroy.

Trust is the foundation of every relationship.

APPRECIATION · TOUCH · TRUST · UNDERSTANDING · DIRE · ENTHUSIASM

Build the foundation. Be the foundation of trust.

When there is trust between two people, miracles can happen. I believe there is no greater experience, no finer feeling than being able to be yourself without being judged, critiqued or mistrusted. When your partner is on the same page as you, trusting you with the same intensity, then love flourishes. And when trust has been broken, the magic stops. We contract and become fearful, mistrusting and doubtful. We all know instinctively when there is trust and when there is not. But what are the elements that build trust? Here are some of the attitudes and behaviors I've seen operating in successful relationships in my practice. These are simple steps you can take to build or rebuild trust in your partnership.

Keep your word … walk your talk.
Tell the truth … always.
Be open … and willing to be vulnerable.
Share your heart … and listen to the others.
Criticize constructively.
Temper your temper.
Surrender graciously.
Understand … and be kind.
–Catherine Cardinal
The 10 Commandments
of Relationships

Trust is the foundation of every relationship.

The glory of friendship is not the outstretched hand, nor the kindly smile, nor the joy of companionship; it is the spiritual inspiration that comes to one when you discover that someone else believes in you and is willing to trust you with a friendship.
–Ralph Waldo Emerson

The value of trust.

Sometimes we wonder how we can build trust in relationships, and know it is hard to survive without it. We want to trust people and want to know how to create it. The golden rule is a good start. That familiar line that we learned as children, "You treat others the way you want to be treated."

Build the foundation. Be the foundation of trust.

I trust you, you trust me, mutual trust brings victory.

Determine the measure of a person by how much you trust them. Believe in them, by how much their life enhances yours.

Let not your heart be troubled: ye believe in God, believe also in me. *–John 14:1 KJV*

I know that the only way to live my life is to try to do what is right, to take the long view, to give of my best in all that the day brings and to put my trust in God. *–Queen Elizabeth, The Times December 26, 2002 front page*

I want the rest of my life to be the best of my life. Worry ends, faith begins. If you worry, you are not trusting. Don't turn the volume down on God when God's silent. He's giving you time to pray.

Faith is trusting God's plan even when you don't understand. Just because you can't read the plans doesn't mean that He hasn't made them. No matter how it looks, He's going to look out for you. Believe that and you'll never go wrong.

To be trusted is a greater compliment than to be loved. Without trust you cannot sustain any kind of relationship.

The Courage To Trust

Adapted from The Stuff of Heroes
William A. Cohen, Longstreet

Sometimes trusting your team is the toughest decision a leader can make. For example, in 1989, Major Clay McCutchan was a gunship pilot supporting ground troops in the U.S. invasion of Panama to capture the dictator Manuel Noriega. On one mission, he was ordered to fire on three armored cars, which were not of the type used by our forces, and about 30 troops near them. Then his crew became convinced the troops were friendly.

McCutchan reviewed what he knew: His ship had sophisticated observation equipment and he trusted his

I will thank God for what I have but I'll trust God for what I need.

very experienced crew to use it. He did not fire—and returned to base expecting to be court-martialed. However, he was proved correct: The troops were Americans who had captured enemy vehicles but lost radio contact. McCutchan had trusted his crew—and saved lives.

Recorded from "Leadership" booklet (Lawrence Ragan Communications)

Sometimes life gets so smoky; we have hurts and troubles.

A Son's Trust

Their home was on fire! The son was inside at the window, but it was so smoky he could not see. The father called for the son to jump into his arms, but the son refused.

The father pleads, "Why won't you jump into my arms?" The son replies, "Daddy, I can't see you!"

Sometimes trusting your team is the toughest decision a leader can make.

So the father explains to him, "That doesn't make any difference. You may not be able to see me, but I can see you! Trust me and jump!" The son does jump and falls comfortably and safely into the father's arms.

Trust Him and take that leap of faith into His arms.

It is the same way with God. We have to have faith and trust Him. Sometimes life gets so smoky; we have hurts and troubles. They may be with relationships or other trials. We get so blinded that we can't see God. But He still sees us. Trust Him and take that leap of faith into His arms.

"I will thank God for what I have but I'll trust God for what I need."

Appreciation

Touch

Trust

Imagination

Time

Understanding

Direction

Enthusiasm

Imagination

A wife said to her husband, "What is it about me that you are most thankful for? Is it my natural beauty, my vivacious personality, or my lavish body?" The husband replied, "I am most thankful for your unbelievable imagination!"

Just imagine!

Imagination is more powerful than knowledge. *–Albert Einstein*

To give anything less than your best is to sacrifice the gift. *–Steve Prefontain*

The world is but a canvas to our imagination. *–Henry David Thoreau*

To give anything less than your best is to sacrifice the gift.

Success requires strength and imagination, energy and persistence.

Imagination keeps kids minds sharp, flexible and open to new opportunities.

Imagination is an internal thought that produces an external result.

Walk in the theatre of your own mind; imagine being, doing and having what God wants you to have for your own life.

"Take time for daydreaming, find a peaceful place, and a few moments to be alone with your thoughts … let your worries float away on the gentle breeze of a cherished dream or a favorite memory … let your imagination wander,

listen as it whispers to you, follow where it invites you to go. Then, slowly, softly, come back to the moment, and return to the world with a touch of daydream magic in your heart.
—*Unknown*

Here are the words to one of our songs. The words describe how we should use our imagination to make our lives better.

"Freedom to Dream"
The Goads

Every child has a wild imagination
Full of wonder that can see beyond the stars
They believe that they can fly
Live in castles in the sky
Every day is an adventure of the heart
Reach back and remember when
nothing held you down

Imagination
is an internal
thought that
produces an
external result.

Chapter 4

There's a spark that lives inside of you
It's still there to be found
The freedom to dream
The freedom to hope
Living with a purpose and a vision
The freedom to try
The freedom to soar
Filled with desire and ambition
Nothing is impossible for you to achieve
When you've got the freedom to dream

Stir up the passion, re-ignite the fire
Build a future, keep your eye on the prize
With the will to persevere
You can overcome your fears
And find a greater purpose for your life
It's time to make a difference, to leave a legacy
Believe in something bigger
And chart your destiny

Now's the time for you to run the race
The limits fall away when you embrace

Appreciation

Touch

Trust

Imagination

Time

Understanding

Direction

Enthusiasm

Time

A man trying to understand the nature of God asked him some questions:

"God, how long is a million years to you?"
And God said, "A million years is like a minute."

Then the man asked, "God, how much is a million dollars to you?"
And God said, "A million dollars is like a penny."

The man thought for a moment and asked, "God, will you give me a penny?"
And God said, "In a minute."
    –Submitted by Lenny Rodin, New York

You punched me pretty hard this morning. I'm just doing my job. Go away and relieve stress this weekend. Then we can start fresh on Monday. *–Sincerely, A. Clock.*

How do you spell love? TIME.

It takes a minute to find a special person,
An hour to appreciate them,
A day to love them,
A lifetime to forget them.

Take time to laugh. It is the music of the soul.

Don't just count the days, make the days count.

The best time to do something significant is between yesterday and tomorrow.

Time is a friend, it is a healer, a maker of dreams. *–Flavia*

Just don't count the days make the days count.

The time is always right to do what's right. If you start your day with these four questions, you'll make every day a more productive day.

1. What's the best thing that can happen today?

2. What's the worst thing that can happen today?

The time is always right to do what's right.

3. What can I do today to make sure that the best thing does happen?

4. What can I do today to make sure that the worst thing does not happen?
–Bits and Pieces October 10, 1996 , page 19

It's time for ordinary men to do extraordinary things. Why settle for something ordinary when God has designed something extraordinary?

Did you ever realize that to be successful it's not how much time you put in – it's what you

The best time to do something significant is between yesterday and tomorrow.

put into the time. Every single day you put in time. You have experiences, everybody does. But not everybody develops expertise. See the difference. You have a choice: you can either GO through an experience or GROW through an experience.

Looking back on the times we've shared together, makes looking ahead even better.

Everyday gets a whole lot better, every time we get together.

Sometimes it doesn't look like we have it all together, but together we have it all.

May the time you give, the hearts you warm, the lives you bless and the sunshine you bring others come back and warm your heart today. Take time to laugh. It is the music of the soul. Take time to think. It is the source of power.

Take time to play. It is the source of perpetual youth.

Take time to read. It is the fountain of wisdom.

Take time to pray. It is the greatest power on earth.

Take time to love and be loved. It is a God-given privilege.

Take time to be friendly. It is the road to happiness.

Take time to give. It is too short a day to be selfish.

Take time to work. It is the price of success.

If you are too BUSY – you are **Being** **Under** **Satan's** **Yoke!**

Everyday gets a whole lot better every time we get together.

You are allowed to have some time for yourself, even if you have to work very hard to find it. Just don't count the time, make the time count. Just don't count

Take time to play. It is the source of perpetual youth.

the days make the days count. Life is short and it can be wrapped up in eight simple words. "If it's to be, it's up to me."

Take time to be friendly. It is the road to happiness.

Most of us spend 58 minutes an hour in living in the past with regret for lost days or shame for things badly done; or in a future which we either long for or dread. The only way to live is to accept each minute as an unrepeatable miracle, which is exactly what it is – a miracle and unrepeatable. –*Margaret S. Jackson*

If you don't stick around for the bad times, you won't be there for the good times.

It's your life, be in it. Now is the time to begin it.

Take time to love and be loved. It is a God-given privilege.

Slow Dance

Have you ever watched kids on a merry-go-round? Or listened to the rain slapping on the ground? Ever followed a butterfly's erotic flight? Or gazed at the sun into the fading night? You better slow down ... don't dance so fast. Time is short. The music won't last. Do you run through each day on the fly? When you ask "how are you" do you hear the reply?

When the day is done, do you lie in bed with the next hundred chores running through your head? You better slow down ... don't dance so fast ... Time is short ... the music won't last.

Ever told your child we'll do it tomorrow and in your haste not see his sorrow? Ever lost touch, let a friendship die because you never had time to call and say hi? You better slow down ... don't dance so fast, time is short ... the music won't last. When you run so fast to get somewhere, you miss half the fun of getting there. When you worry and hurry through the day. It is like an unopened gift thrown away. Life is not a race … do take it slower, hear the music before the song is over! –*Unknown*

Slow Me Down, Lord
And He said unto them, Come ye yourselves apart into a desert place, and rest a while: for there were many coming and going, and they had no leisure so much as to eat.
–*Mark 6:31 KJV*

Or as someone else has said, "Come apart and rest a while before you come apart!"

I remember years ago writing the saying on my desk, "Beware of the barrenness of a busy life!" I think in our day and age so many of us struggle with being too busy. I certainly do. It is a constant battle.

I found this prayer by *Wilferd Arlan Peterson* that may help you slow down:

Ease the pounding of my heart by the quieting of my mind. Steady my hurried pace. Give me, amidst the day's confusion, the calmness of the everlasting hills.

Break the tensions of my nerves and muscles with the soothing music of singing streams that live in my memory.

Help me to know the magical, restoring power of sleep. Teach me the art of taking "minute vacations" ... slowing down to look at a flower, to chat with a friend, to read a few lines from a good book.

Remind me of the fable of the hare and the tortoise; that the race is not always to the swift; that there is more to life than measuring its speed. Let me look up at the branches of the towering oak and know that it grew slowly and well. Inspire me to send my own roots down deep into the soil of life's endearing values ... that I may grow toward the stars of my greater destiny.

Slow me down, Lord.

LIFE'S CLOCK

Life's clock is wound but once,
and no man hath the power
to know where the hands will stop
at late or early hour.

To lose one's wealth is sad indeed,
To lose one's health is more,
To lose one's soul is such a loss
that no man can restore.
Today only is our own,
so live, love and toil with a will.
Place no faith in tomorrow
for the clock may soon be still.

—Darlene Virginia Quarles

Each day is a new account ...

- If you had a bank that credited your account each morning with $86,400

- That carried over no balance from day to day …

- Allowed you to keep no cash in your account …

- And every evening canceled whatever part of the amount you had failed to use during the day …

- What would you do?

- Draw out every cent every day, of course, and use it to your advantage!

- Well, you have such a bank … and its name is "TIME." Every morning, it credits you with 86,400 seconds.

Take time
to give. It is too
short a day
to be selfish.

- Every night, it rules off as lost whatever of this you have failed to invest to good purpose.

- It carries over no balances.

- It allows no overdrafts.

- Each day, it opens a new account with you.

- Each night, it burns the records of the day.

- If you fail to use the day's deposits, the loss is yours.

- There is no going back.

- There is no drawing against to "Tomorrow."

- It is up to each of us to invest this precious fund of hours, minutes, and seconds in order to get from it the utmost in health, happiness and success!
  –Anonymous

Appreciation

Touch

Trust

Imagination

Time

Understanding

Direction

Enthusiasm

CHAPTER 6

Understanding

Wisdom is the principal thing; therefore get wisdom: and with all thy getting get understanding. *—Proverbs 4:7 KJV*

When someone is grieving, they're not looking for answers; they are looking for love and encouragement and understanding.

Maybe if you did a better job of listening, history wouldn't have to repeat itself. Listening is love in action.
—Bits and Pieces on Leadership

The first rule of love is listening and understanding.

THE CRACKED POT

I love this story of the cracked pot that I received in an email. I don't know who wrote it, but it illustrates the power of understanding.

A water bearer in India had two large pots; each hung on each end of a pole which he carried across his neck. One of the pots had a crack in it, and while the other pot was perfect and always delivered a full portion of water at the end of the long walk from the stream to the master's house, the cracked pot arrived only half full.

For a full two years this went on daily, with the bearer delivering only one and a half pots full of water to his master's house. Of course, the perfect pot was proud of its accomplishments, perfect to the end for which it was made. But the poor cracked pot was ashamed of its own imperfection, and miserable that it was able to accomplish only half of what it had been made to do.

After two years of what it perceived to be a bitter failure, it spoke to the water bearer one day by the stream.

"I am ashamed of myself, and I want to apologize to you."

"Why?" asked the bearer. "What are you ashamed of?"

"I have been able, for these past two years, to deliver only half my load because this crack in my side causes water to leak out all the way back to your master's house. Because of my flaws, you have to do all of this work, and you don't get full value from your efforts," the pot said.

The water bearer felt sorry for the old cracked pot, and in his compassion he said, "As we return to the master's house, I want you to notice the beautiful flowers along the path."

The only time we should look down on somebody is to lift them up.

Indeed, as they went up the hill, the old cracked pot took notice of the sun warming the beautiful wild flowers on the side of the path, and this cheered it some. But at the end of the trail, it still felt bad because it had leaked out half its load, and so again it apologized to the bearer for its failure.

The bearer said to the pot, "Did you notice that there were flowers only on your side of your path, but not on the other pot's side? That's because I have always known about your flaw, and I took advantage of it. I planted flower seeds on your side of the path, and every day while we walk back from the stream, you've watered them. For two years I have been able to pick these beautiful flowers to decorate my master's table. Without you being just the way you are, he would not have this beauty to grace his house."

Each of us has our own unique flaws. We're all cracked pots. But when we understand our flaws and others... take advantage of them. Knowing that in our weakness there is beauty in our pathways.

There's one more story about understanding that I would like to share with you. It touched my heart and I hope it touches yours.

About ten years ago, a young and very successful executive named Josh was traveling down a Chicago neighborhood street. He was going a bit too fast in his sleek black Jaguar, which was only two months old.

He was watching for kids darting out from between parked cars and slowed down when he thought he saw something. As his car passed, no child darted out, but a brick hurled out and–WHUMP!–it smashed into the Jag's shiny black side door! SCREECH!!!! Brakes slammed! Gears ground into reverse, and tires madly spun the Jaguar back to the spot from where the brick had been thrown.

Josh jumped out of the car, grabbed the kid and pushed him up against a parked car. He shouted at the kid, "What was that all about and who are you? Just

Know that in our weakness there is beauty in our pathways.

what the heck are you doing?!" Building up a head of steam, he went on. "That's my new Jag, and that brick you threw is gonna cost you a lot of money. Why did you throw it?"

"Please, mister, please … I'm sorry! I didn't know what else to do!" Pleaded the youngster. "I threw the brick because no one else would stop!" Tears were dripping down the boy's chin as he pointed around the parked car.

"It's my brother, mister," he said. "He rolled off the curb and fell out of his wheelchair and I can't lift him up." Sobbing, the boy asked the executive,

The first
rule of love
is listening and
understanding.

"Would you please help me get him back into his wheelchair? He's hurt and he's too heavy for me."

Moved beyond words, the young executive tried desperately to swallow the rapidly swelling lump in his throat. Straining, he lifted the young man back into the wheelchair, took out his handkerchief and wiped the scrapes and cuts, checking to see that everything was going to be OK. He then watched the younger brother push him down the sidewalk toward their home.

It was a long walk back to the sleek, black, shining, Jaguar … a long and slow walk. Josh never did fix the side door of his Jaguar. He kept the dent to remind him that there are times in our lives when we think we understand, and we don't. We have to be stopped, and although it is not always pleasant, it can be worth it to understand those around us and the little things we can do to make someone's life better.

The only time we should look down on somebody is to lift them up.

Appreciation

Touch

Trust

Imagination

Time

Understanding

Direction

Enthusiasm

CHAPTER 7

Direction

Life is a journey. It sure helps if you are going in the right direction.

It is not where you stand, but the direction you're going in.

Correction with direction equals protection.

Desire + dedication with direction = destiny.

Find people that believe in you and encourage you to go down the right path.

Sometimes life's detours can take you exactly where you need to go.

Momentum happens once you are moving in the direction of your goals. Nothing can stop you.

APPRECIATION · TOUCH · TRUST · IN
UNDERSTANDING · DIREC
NTHUSIASM

Direction

If you never face the devil you are probably heading in the same direction.

Live simply.
Love generously.
Care deeply.
Speak kindly.
Leave the rest to God.

When God's word changes the direction of your life, that change is the turning point to an encouraging new beginning.

Your life always moves in the direction of your dominant thought.

Funny how we are so quick to take direction from a total stranger when we are lost, but are hesitant to take God's direction to be found. I was reading about the medieval torturing method called "Quartering". A man's arms and legs were tied to four different horses. When the command was given, the horses took off in four different directions. The person was literally quartered–torn to pieces. I thought of this when a man was discussing with me the fragmentation of his own life. I know the feeling, don't you?

Find people that believe in you and encourage you to go down the right path.

There are so many lives we want to live. So many paths we want to travel. How can you get anywhere when strange inner yearnings call you this way and that, and sometimes they are in direct conflict to one another?

Focus is like a compass–it keeps you pointed in the right direction. If you keep changing your direction, you will never reach your destiny.

If one advances confidently in the direction of his dreams, and endeavors to live life which he has

Your life always moves in the direction of your dominant thought.

imagined, he will meet with success unexpected in common hours. —*Henry David Thoreau*

You've got to think about big things while you're doing small things, so that all the small things go in the right direction." —*Alvin Toffler*

Sometimes in the winds of change we find our true direction.

The average person takes 19,002 steps daily—many in the wrong direction.

Heroes and cowards are doing the same thing; they're both afraid and they're both running, but heroes are running in the right direction.

GEESE

We have all seen the beautiful sight of flocks of geese heading South for the winter, flying along in their "V" formation.   It is interesting to note that scientists for many years have found this behavior worthy of study.   Millions of dollars and thousands of hours of research have gone into telling us the following:

As each bird flaps its wings, it creates an uplift for the bird immediately following.   By flying in a "V" formation, the flock (as a whole) adds approximately 71% greater flying range than if each bird flew on its own.

People who are part of a team and share a common direction get where they are going quicker and easier, because they are traveling on the trust of one another.

Whenever a goose falls out of formation,

it suddenly feels the drag and resistance of trying to go through it alone and quickly gets back into formation to take advantage of the power of the flock.

If we have as much sense as a goose, we will seek out information and support from those who are headed in the same direction we are going. When the lead goose gets tired, he rotates back in the wing and another goose takes over.

It pays to share leadership and take turns doing the hard jobs. The geese honk from behind to encourage those at the head to keep up their speed. Words of support and inspiration help energize those on the front line, helping them keep pace in spite of the day-to-day pressures and fatigue.

Finally, when a goose gets sick or is wounded and must fall out of formation, two geese fall out of the formation and follow the injured bird down to help and protect him. They stay with him until he is either able to fly or until he is dead. In the event of his death, the geese join another formation to catch up with their group.

Sometimes in the winds of change we find our true direction.

If we have the sense of a goose, we will stand by each other when things get rough. The next time you see a formation of geese, remember …

It is a reward and a challenge to be a contributing member of a team and you can all help each other to go in the right direction.
–Author Unknown

Direction determines destination, so here is a question that you must ask yourself. Are all of my disciplines taking me where I want to go?
–Jim Rohn

Appreciation

Touch

Trust

Imagination

Time

Understanding

Direction

Enthusiasm

Enthusiasm

Your enthusiasm inspires people.

Enthusiasm makes ordinary people extraordinary.
–Unknown

Enthusiasm is the awareness that every new beginning begins in darkness.

Success is going from failure to failure without losing your enthusiasm. *–Abraham Lincoln*

I know that I'm an optimist because I can put the "fun" in dysfunctional.

Enthusiasm finds the opportunities, and energy makes the most of them.
–Henry S. Haskins, Bits and Pieces

Enthusiasm

Nothing is so contagious as enthusiasm; it moves stones, it charms brutes. Enthusiasm is the genius of sincerity, and truth accomplishes no victories without it.
–*Edward GE Bulwer Lytton, Bits and Pieces*

Every morning when I look in the mirror and get over the initial shock, I wonder if it is the same man I put to bed the night before … I look in the mirror and tell myself "I'm alive, alert, awake, joyful and enthusiastic about my day!"

May the fleas of a thousand camels infect the armpits of the person that tries to screw up my day and may God make their arms too short to scratch them.

An extraordinary person is an ordinary person that has tenacity and determination. He doesn't pray for a lighter load, he prays for a stronger back. And those that have the character to carry out the plan even after the initial burst of enthusiasm is gone. They are persistent and know they have to hang in there when everything inside of them says to let go. That's an extraordinary person.

The worst bankrupt is the man who has lost his enthusiasm. Let a man lose everything in the world but his enthusiasm and he will come through again to success. To keep full of enthusiasm, keep your intake of energy greater than the outgo of energy. *–Norman Vincent Peale*

An optimist is one who takes cold water thrown upon his idea, heats it up with enthusiasm, and uses the steam to push ahead!

Someone asked the conductor of a great symphony orchestra which instrument he considered the most difficult to play. "Second fiddle," said the conductor. "I can get plenty of

Enthusiasm
is the awareness
that every new
beginning begins
in darkness.

first violinists, but to find one who can play second fiddle with enthusiasm – that's a problem. And if we have no second fiddle, we have no harmony!" It is hard to have harmony with everybody singing the same note.

Enthusiasm is one of the most powerful engines of success. When you do a thing, do it with your might. Put your whole soul into it. Stamp it with your own personality. Be active, be energetic, be enthusiastic and faithful, and you will accomplish your object. Nothing great was ever achieved without enthusiasm.
–*Ralph Waldo Emerson, Bits and Pieces*
March 31, 1994

Enthusiasm comes from the Greek words, "En Theos," meaning "In God." So when you are enthusiastic, that very attitude is evidence of God's presence in you.

Ending Comments

I want you to remember, the world needs more people like you. People who are willing to leave things a little better than they found them. People who reach out with compassion. People who are willing to put all selfishness aside to do the good, right, kind thing–just because they know it will make a difference someday to someone. This world needs more people like you.

I hope you enjoyed this book! There is much more to come in future volumes. Please feel free to contact me and let me know what you think.

Curt

Curt Goad Ministries, Inc.
PO Box 771390
Orlando, Florida 32877
321.233.1500
www.curtgoad.com

$\mathcal{N}$othing can prevent the person with the right mental attitude from achieving success and nothing on earth can help a person with the wrong attitude.

You live
only once,
but once is
enough if
you live right.

Encouragement

THE ABC's

APPRECIATION · TOUCH · TRUST · IMAGINATION

TIME · UNDERSTANDING · DIRECTION

ENTHUSIASM

A

IS FOR ATTITUDE

About the Author

Curt Goad remembers two things that defined his life as a young boy …

First: in school, he used to talk out of turn all the time. The teacher spoke to his mother about the problem. Curt's mom sat him down and told him, "God's given you a wonderful gift. Now we'll have to pray to God to show you how to use it." The next day at school Curt was very quiet. Curious, his teacher asked him why he was so quiet. He responded, "My mom says I have a gift and now's not the time to use it." Today Curt does use that gift as he speaks to both large and small groups, giving words of wisdom through his quotes, humor and stories.

Secondly: at the age of 6 he started singing with his family in churches. Today, he's still singing. Curt, one of "The Goads", primarily performs with his brother and sister. Over the years they have sung for millions of people throughout the world.

Curt's goal is not to try to get people to think their way into better living, but to live their way into better thinking. He has always wanted to encourage people to be better than they thought they could be. Whether that be through a smile, a story, a song, a prayer or a hug, Curt looks at his job as the chance to do whatever it takes to make peoples lives better. He says, "There is no respecter of persons, everyone needs encouragement. And I want to do whatever I can to give that to them."

Curt Goad has also authored two other books. *Getting Started Right*, a book for new believers in the Christian faith and *Little Book of Encouragement* which gives you the hope to turn adversity into the stepping stones to success.

Have a great day, it's yours to enjoy!